for·ward /ˈfôrwərd/

Adverb

toward the front, onward so as to make progress; toward a successful conclusion

Adjective

facing toward the front, relating to or concerned with the future

Verb

send on to a further destination, help to advance

FORWARD

MAN'S GUIDE TO HEALING AND THRIVING THROUGH DIVORCE

DR. BROOKS TILLER

First Printing, 2023
ISBN 979-8-9898276-7-1

Edited by Benjamin Richardson
Book Layout and Design by Brent Spears

www.DrBrooksTiller.com

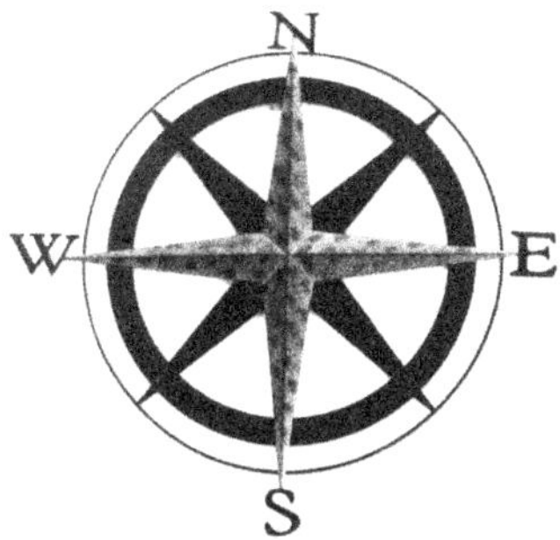

When facing the challenges of divorce, we have an important decision to make. We can either stay stuck in the past or consciously embrace the unknown and move forward. Staying in our comfort zone may be tempting. Yet, true bravery is achieved by moving forward through discomfort. We should keep our eyes on the possibility of a better future.

Forward, we must go, evolving for ourselves, our loved ones, and those who care for us. On this journey, we will encounter difficult paths and intimidating unknowns. We will rediscover the man we were created to be through our struggles. Moving forward, each small step is a giant stride toward transformation. We're leaving the bleak, dark, lonely valley and heading towards the triumphant peak. Our ascent awaits us.

Moving forward requires resilience. It is an essential journey to self-discovery and a better future.

In this earthly life, we inevitably experience wounds along our journey —cuts, bruises, and brokenness that make us bleed as we traverse the wilderness. Divorce inflicts wounds that may not be visible externally, but deeply affect our hearts and souls, stemming from the separation of our sacred marital vows. This disconnection can lead to isolation as we grapple with our wounds.

Divorce, the choice to end a once-promising marital bond, resembles a wound that severs the intimate connection between two souls. It creates a void where unity once thrived, with emotional wounds that leave us exposed and sensitive. Divorce can leave us feeling as if a piece of us has been forcibly torn away. Just as a physical wound requires attention, cleansing, nurturing, and time to heal, moving on from divorce necessitates tending to and healing emotional, mental, and spiritual wounds.

Adding to the complexity, we find ourselves lost in a dark valley within the wilderness. Amidst the darkness, feeling isolated and far from familiar comforts, caring for our wounds can prove challenging. Nevertheless, it's crucial to stop the bleeding and provide proper care, enabling us to move forward and heal.

Failure to address the wound could lead to further harm – we risk bleeding out, rendering us incapable of aiding others. While we need assistance from others to halt the bleeding and initiate healing, it's imperative that we also permit others to help us mend the wound.

However, we can't embark on the healing process until we acknowledge and assess the wound. Only then can we treat it effectively, applying a metaphorical tourniquet to halt the bleeding and allow the healing process to commence.

The healing journey after a divorce demands time and effort. We must delve deep into our souls, honestly assessing our needs. Occasionally, the wound may become infected, requiring us to cleanse and open it to facilitate proper healing. Healing is a gradual process, but with dedicated care, support from others, and God's guidance and grace, we can find solace in the journey.

We can heal.
We have the ability to heal.
Healing is within our reach.
This journal will serve as a companion in the healing journey.

These journal prompts are designed to help you process your emotions, seek guidance from God, and navigate the complexities of divorce. They can aid in healing your wounds, in self-reflection on who God needs you to be, and strengthen your faith during this challenging season.

This journal will serve us as a daily practice as we walk through this dark valley. Each day will begin with a quick read to challenge, encourage, and uplift us. Following the reading, we have a journal prompt with a space for us to write. Finally, there are a few verses of scripture for further study and reflection.

This is not an easy time. It is not a time to take it easy. It is taking action and moving forward that gets us from this dark valley to a better and brighter future.

This journal is not an ordinary journal. This is a journey. A journey that is not traveled alone. We are on this journey together.

Read it. Soak it in. Then, do the work.

This journal is our way of getting it out. Our way of acknowledging and assessing the wound is to address it adequately and allow it to heal.

Wounds are nasty; scars are sexy!

Let's get to stepping and moving forward.

GUIDANCE

Divorce casts a lonely shadow over the path we tread. Yet, it's a journey we need not undertake in solitude. The presence of companions, even in the darkest valleys, brings a measure of reassurance. The fear, although shared, can become profoundly intimidating when faced alone.

This journal is a journey that we are taking together. We will be walking this path together and looking to God as our ultimate guide.

Amidst the assistance of others, it's vital to recognize that our ultimate refuge lies in God. His guidance alone can steer us through this storm, offering a solace that transcends human comfort.

Embarking on the Quest for Divine Direction: Reflect upon how you've turned to God for guidance during this intricate journey. Record moments of prayer and instances where insights from the Bible have illuminated your path. By documenting these experiences, you honor the role of faith in navigating life's challenges.

Proverbs 3:5-6
Psalm 32:8

EMOTIONS

Most of what floods our mind at first is pain - emotional pain. Parts of our identity and life have been ripped away, and now we are left with a gaping wound. It hurts more than any physical pain your body has ever felt.

As men, we may have been conditioned not to recognize our emotions. Or, we associate emotions with weakness, so we suppress and ignore them. Emotions are natural, yet they do not get to control or even dictate our response.

The first step we must take is to acknowledge and understand them. Emotions inform us, but they do not rule us. We get to decide how we respond to our emotions. If we understand them, they can provide us with discernment and insights that we can use to stop the hurting and survive logically.

Walking through the wilderness, we could suffer a terrible fall, breaking an arm and leaving us profusely bleeding. We could lie down and writhe in pain. We could sit in our tent feeling sorry for ourselves. We could watch the blood pour until we bleed out. Or, we can use the pain to figure out what injured us, how badly we are hurt, and what actions we must take to survive.

Like the pain that tells us that our bodies have been physically wounded, emotions provide critical information. Emotions tell us how we have been hurt and what to do.

We then decide how we take informed action and respond appropriately.

Face the fact that the emotions we are feeling right here, right now, are real!

Reflect on your emotions: How have you felt since the divorce began? Acknowledge and name your emotions. Write about your experiences and the emotions that have surfaced.

Psalm 34:18
Philippians 4:6-7
James 1:19-20

GRATITUDE

Gratitude is often associated with joy, happiness, and the positive aspects of life. However, it's vital to distinguish gratitude from merely counting our blessings one by one.

In the midst of this wilderness, where our souls feel battered and bleeding, it might appear counterintuitive to find gratitude. How can we muster gratitude when we're standing alone in the desolation of divorce, our hearts broken and spirits wounded?

This isn't the place we intended to find ourselves in, and the journey ahead is far from easy. It's not picturesque; in fact, there is no denying this journey is marked by complex challenges. Presently, the ability to tally up blessings might seem scarce, and cultivating gratitude might feel like a challenge in and of itself. But even amidst these hardships, if we take a pause to step back and look around, we can uncover blessings and find a reason to be grateful.

Studies show that gratitude has a positive impact on our health - physical, mental, spiritual, and emotional. Gratitude allows us to appreciate and focus on what we have instead of looking at what we do not have. Science has shown that gratitude improves well-being, improves relationships, improves sleep, improves immune function, improves resiliency, decreases stress, and even lowers blood pressure.

Discovering Gratitude amid Challenges: Reflect on three things you can express gratitude for today, even as you navigate the complexities of divorce.

Start each day with "I am grateful for ……." then let your pen flow.

Psalm 100:4
I Thessalonians 5:18
Colossians 3:15

TRUSTING GOD'S PLAN

Some people will try to provide solace and reassurance by stating, "It's God's will." Although their intentions are good, these words can be painful, perplexing, and discouraging. God doesn't want us to be afflicted with sickness or to suffer an injury. In the same manner, divorce was never part of God's intention.

Yet, even from our worst circumstances, positive results can arise through the intervention and power of God. He can utilize our challenges and hardships to bring about good, to bring glory, and to offer support to others — provided we allow ourselves to be instruments in His hands.

While this may not have been a part of God's explicit blueprint, He can incorporate it into His grand design for our lives. If we allow God to use us and this dark valley of divorce we are in, He can help us to become more like the man He created us to be.

Relying on Divine Guidance: Reflect on how your faith has been a guiding light during this demanding phase. Chronicle instances where you've discerned God's influence actively shaping events.

Proverbs 3:5-6
Jeremiah 29:11
Romans 8:28

FORGIVING

Peter once questioned Jesus about forgiveness, proposing forgiving someone up to seven times. Admittedly, this seems generous, and one might assume that the other person would grasp the lesson by then. However, Jesus's response surpasses this notion by urging Peter to forgive seventy times seven.

To put it into perspective, this equates to forgiving someone once daily for approximately a year and a half. This frequency might appear overwhelming, and indeed, it is. Essentially, we are called to cultivate an ongoing spirit of forgiveness.

Forgiveness presents a formidable challenge, particularly while navigating the complexities of divorce. Extending forgiveness to those who have caused us pain and are responsible for our wounds is undoubtedly no easy feat. Nonetheless, at this moment, embracing forgiveness stands as a crucial instrument for our healing journey.

Forgiving is critical. Yet, at this stage, we may be unable to communicate it or even be welcome to share our forgiveness with those we forgive. Yet, we can still forgive, even if we cannot speak the words to them.

Journey of Forgiveness: Consider the concept of forgiveness and its relevance to your divorce journey. Are there specific areas where you recognize the need to offer forgiveness to others?

Matthew 6:14-15
Colossians 3:13
Ephesians 4:31-32

FORGIVING OURSELVES

Forgiveness is a profound act that often carries a surprising truth: its true beneficiary is the man looking back at us in the mirror. When we choose to forgive, we unburden our hearts and minds, freeing ourselves from the weight of anger and resentment. Conversely, holding onto grievances is like tightly gripping burning embers — it scorches us from within. Drinking the poison of anger with hopes that it harms others only ends up poisoning us, leading to our suffering.

Today is a reminder that self-forgiveness is essential. Some of the wounds and battle scars that we carry inevitably come from our own hands at times. Throughout our journey in this life, none of us will emerge unscathed; we all require moments of forgiveness. It's crucial to extend the same compassion we offer others to ourselves.

Grant yourself the kindness and forgiveness you deserve today.

Self-Forgiveness Reflection: Reflect on areas where you've struggled to forgive yourself and take a pen to paper to compose a note brimming with genuine self-forgiveness. Embrace the healing it can bring, nurturing your path toward self-acceptance and growth.

Psalm 103:10-12
I John 1:9

HEALING

Divorce inflicts a painful rupture, tearing apart two souls that God once united. The resulting wounds are far from attractive; they're raw and unpleasant. Left untreated, they fester, inviting infection, and compounding our troubles.

The process of healing is a fluctuating one, characterized by its highs and lows. We might feel empowered to face the world one moment, only to have an unexpected trigger strip away the cover, exposing the tender wound to every element in the room.

There's a temptation to press forward, to ignore the wound, but this approach only invites infection. Left unchecked, the infection spreads, affecting multiple aspects of our lives. It's crucial to address these wounds, not just the physical ones, but the spiritual, mental, and emotional ones we endure.

During this critical phase, seeking proper healing is paramount. While it might be tempting to turn to vices as a temporary escape from the pain, it's like trying to cover a bullet hole with tape — ineffective and potentially worsening the situation. True healing requires us to pause and genuinely tend to the wound.

God stands ready to offer the healing we need if we turn to Him. He can mend our brokenness, restore our strength, and guide us through this healing journey. While the healing process may be lengthy and arduous, it transforms wounds into scars. And those scars, a testament to our resilience, carry a unique beauty.

Nurtured by Divine Love: Reflect on your journey of healing. Write about how you're discovering strength and renewal through your connection with God's love. Describe moments where you've felt His presence guiding you towards restoration. Through your words, you acknowledge the power of faith in the process of recovery.

Psalm 147:3
Jeremiah 30:17

BAND OF BROTHERS

The iconic lines, "We few, we happy few, we band of brothers," spoken by King Henry in Shakespeare's Henry V, encapsulate a spirit of camaraderie and unity. This stirring speech was addressed to those ready to stand and fight. Individuals prepared to charge into battle even when vastly outnumbered. These were comrades willing to lay it all on the line for the sake of their fellow soldiers.

In our challenging times, a strong band of brothers is equally crucial. These are men we can rely upon, lean on, and find support from. They're the ones who extend a helping hand and guide us along the difficult path. These are individuals we trust deeply, with whom we can share our struggles, and confront trials openly and honestly.

Our band of brothers is there to help us stop the bleeding. They hold the bandage in place. They can pick us up when we fall down and even carry us to safety when we are wounded and unable to walk. Lean into these men and let them help to stop the bleeding and heal our wounds.

The Power of Community: Reflect on the significance of community and relationships during this trying phase. Consider individuals who have stood by you and offered their support. Explore ways in which you can reach out to others for assistance. Compile a list of men you can connect with, fostering a genuine band of brothers—a network that brings strength, encouragement, and shared understanding. By nurturing these connections, you create a foundation of support that can help carry you through the challenges you face.

Ecclesiastes 4:9-10
Proverbs 27:17

RECLAIMING IDENTITY

Amid the upheaval of divorce, our sense of self is profoundly shaken, leaving us with shattered remnants of the identity we once knew. The future we had meticulously mapped out has dissolved into thin air, leaving us adrift in uncertainty. The image we had of ourselves has become a fleeting mirage, and the certainty we held dear has crumbled away.

Doubt creeps in, self-questioning takes hold, and we find ourselves in a disorienting place where our purpose feels elusive. The sensation of not knowing who we truly are can be overwhelming. Like a warrior who has lost a limb, we feel the large gaping wound in our soul as we have been torn apart.

Yet, during this turmoil, one constant remains: our identity as a child of God. Despite any external perceptions or internal struggles, we are cherished creations, desired and redeemed through the ultimate sacrifice of Jesus.

This knowledge is a comforting anchor—proof that we are cherished, loved, and valued by God. It's a reminder that our worth and identity are rooted in our relationship with Jesus Christ. God's love can fill the hole in our soul and stop the bleeding.

Reconstructing Identity: Reflect on how the divorce has influenced your sense of self. Take time to journal about the process of rediscovering your identity in Christ and the renewed purpose that lies ahead. Through this reflection, you can find solace in your spiritual foundation and uncover the path toward embracing your identity anew.

2 Corinthians 5:17
Ephesians 2:10

POWER OF SCRIPTURE

The Word of God holds an unmatched power — capable of not only healing our brokenness but also transforming our lives. It is a guiding force, a beacon that lights our path even through the darkest storms.

Scripture serves as a reliable compass, offering direction when we're lost and assurance when we're faltering. Psalm 34:18 extends comfort, unveiling God's enduring love and nearness: "The Lord is close to the brokenhearted. He saves those whose spirits have been crushed." (Psalm 34:18 ICB)

In times of weakness, God's strength becomes our support, as Isaiah 41:10 reminds us: "So don't worry, because I am with you. Don't be afraid, because I am your God. I will make you strong and will help you. I will support you with my right hand that saves you." (Isaiah 41:10 ICB)

Paradoxically, it's when we're at our weakest that Christ's strength shines brightest. Recognizing our limitations and vulnerabilities, we come to realize that it's His power that carries us through each day, giving us victory over our struggles. As 2 Corinthians 12:9-10 teaches: "My grace is all you need. My power works best in weakness... when I am weak, then I am truly strong." (2 Corinthians 12:9-10 NLT)

Jesus encouraged us not to be consumed by worry but rather to trust Him to provide and care for us. "So don't worry about tomorrow. Each day has enough trouble of its own. Tomorrow will have its own worries." (Matthew 6:34 ICB)

Allow God's Word to be the ointment and bandage that we need to heal our wound of divorce. Pour into scripture and watch how the Lord will work in us, on us, and through us to heal and make us whole again.

Reflecting on the Power of Scripture: Take time to document specific Bible verses that bring you comfort and guidance during the challenges of divorce. Write them down and display them where you can see and read them regularly. By immersing yourself in these verses, you cultivate a connection to God's wisdom and strength, allowing His words to shape your perspective and fortify your spirit throughout this season.

Hebrews 4:12
Psalm 119:105

LETTING GO

The desire for control is a natural instinct, yet the irony lies in that the tighter we cling, the more elusive our grasp becomes. Our attempts to manage everything often result in us losing our grip even faster. The illusion of control breeds chaos rather than order.

It's crucial to come to terms with the reality of our limited control. While it's simpler to list what we can control, acknowledging what we cannot control is equally important. Our sphere of influence is primarily within ourselves—our actions, words, and choices.

To find peace, we must release our grip and recognize the necessity of surrendering to God's providence. Trying to seize control can be likened to wresting the steering wheel from God's hands, a futile endeavor that often leads to unfavorable outcomes.

Embracing Surrender: Take time to reflect on the areas of control you need to relinquish and entrust to God. How can you abandon your plans and yield to His divine design for your life? Through this reflection, you acknowledge your humility and cultivate a deeper connection to God's guidance, finding solace in surrender rather than resistance.

Philippians 4:6-7
Matthew 11:28-30

REDISCOVER PASSIONS

Remember the days when we were deeply engaged in hobbies and passions? There was a time when our interests brought us immense joy. However, amidst the turbulence of divorce, it's understandable that our focus has narrowed to the seismic shifts in our lives.

But, merely dwelling on the challenges won't propel us forward. It's time to take action to venture out of our comfort zones. Let's revisit those activities that once sparked our enthusiasm. Give new hobbies a shot to rejuvenate our mind, body, and soul.

Consider exploring a running club, where the rhythm of each step can mirror your journey of healing. Or perhaps, join a rec basketball league—a physical outlet that embodies teamwork and camaraderie. The simplicity of camping can reconnect you with nature's tranquility, while a fishing trip offers solitude and connection with fellow anglers. Alternatively, card games, checkers, or chess can stimulate your mind and foster social interaction.

Rediscovery and Rejuvenation: Document the activities or interests that resonate with you and bring joy. Reflect on how you can reintegrate them into your life post-divorce. Please choose one of these endeavors and immerse yourself in it, noting how it makes you feel and considering ways to incorporate more of such experiences into your life. By pursuing these passions, you carve out spaces of fulfillment and contentment amid the challenges you're navigating.

Psalm 37:4
Ecclesiastes 3:1

BOUNDARIES

The dissolution of our marriage often triggers us to reevaluate all our relationships—family, friends, acquaintances, and colleagues. While it's natural to scrutinize these connections during such a period, it's important not to isolate ourselves. Instead, we can seize the opportunity to reflect on the quality of our relationships and cultivate healthier connections.

This juncture allows us to assess which relationships contribute positively to our lives and which might not be beneficial. Taking the time to differentiate between the two is crucial. Establishing clear boundaries becomes a powerful tool in maintaining healthy connections, ensuring that we surround ourselves with individuals who respect and honor those boundaries.

In this process, it's vital to recognize that our boundaries are not for others; they are for us. Boundaries safeguard our well-being and create spaces where we can flourish. Boundaries give us room and space to heal and recover from our wounds. As we set boundaries, we empower ourselves to foster relationships that uplift us and steer away from those that infringe upon our mental, emotional, and spiritual health.

Navigating New Relationship Dynamics: Reflect on how friendships and family relationships have shifted in the wake of divorce. Embrace the idea that our boundaries are a personal investment in our well-being. Explore strategies for nurturing healthy connections and setting boundaries that align with your needs and values. Through this exploration, you pave the way for relationships that bring out the best in you and support your growth.

We must establish our boundaries. Write about ways to maintain healthy connections and set boundaries.

Proverbs 4:23
I Corinthians 6:19-20

GRIEVING

Grieving the end of our marriage is a painful yet essential part of the healing journey. Permitting ourselves to truly feel the weight of sorrow and loss is a necessary step in navigating the aftermath of divorce. This painful process involves tearing souls apart, leaving a wound that requires acknowledgment and time for healing.

Properly addressing our grief, just like properly caring for a wound, is crucial. Experts on grief have listed various stages of grief that we process and walk through. In real life it's important to recognize grieving is not a linear or uniform process. Some frameworks outline five steps, and others even more, such as:

1.   Shock
2.   Denial
3.   Anger
4.   Bargaining
5.   Depression
6.   Acceptance
7.   Hope

These stages aren't always experienced in a neat sequence. They can intertwine and fluctuate, and we may progress through them in different orders or even circle back to earlier stages. The key is that we grieve and continue to move forward.

Self-Honesty in the Healing Journey: Take a moment to reflect on the stages of grief you may have encountered so far during your divorce journey. Acknowledge your feelings—shock, denial, anger, bargaining, depression, acceptance, and hope. Grieving is a personal and evolving process, and recognizing where you stand on this path can offer insight into your healing and growth. Acknowledging your grief, you're taking a significant step towards nurturing your well-being and finding a renewed sense of purpose.

Psalm 34:18
Matthew 5:4

PEACE

Finding peace amidst the challenges of divorce can indeed be a daunting task. The waves of uncertainty and upheaval threaten to overwhelm our hearts and minds. Yet, just as Jesus calmed the storm for the apostles with the words, "Peace be still," we also can receive peace during turmoil.

Often, our struggle to find peace arises from being consumed by the waves of the past and the fear of future storms. The remedy lies in embracing serenity in the present moment. Focusing on the here and now allows us to release the grip of the past and entrust the unfolding future to God.

True peace isn't the absence of turmoil; it's a quiet strength that resides within us, offering resilience. To access this wellspring of peace, we must release bitterness, anger, and shame, inviting God's love, grace, mercy, joy, and peace to fill the void. As we anchor our thoughts in gratitude and growth, we find a foundation of tranquility.

Faith becomes our anchor, and the company of uplifting individuals becomes a source of strength. In introspection and embracing connection, a peace that transcends divorce's challenges awaits.

Amidst the overwhelming moments, remember the serenity prayer—a powerful reminder of acceptance, courage, and wisdom.

Taking a Pause for Stillness: Research indicates that 17 minutes of stillness can cultivate focus and calmness. Set aside 20 minutes to lie down, embracing quietude. Please pay attention to your breath, allowing it to ground you in the present. If your mind drifts to past pain or future worries, gently guide it back to the present moment, focusing only on your breath. As you engage in this practice, remember, "Be still and know that I am God." After this time, write down how you feel, capturing the essence of presence and peace in your reflections.

Philippians 4:6-7
Isaiah 26:3

SELF CARE

The pre-flight safety briefing on airplanes reminds us of a critical principle: before aiding others, we must secure our well-being by putting on our oxygen masks first. In the journey through divorce, the same principle applies—we must ensure our self-care is in place.

Amidst the emotional turmoil, it's all too easy to neglect ourselves. Days may pass without proper nourishment, and sleep may elude us, leading to unproductive days. The isolation can make us hesitant to venture outside, and the emotional weight can cloud our connection with God.

It's paramount that we prioritize our well-being. Just as an airplane's oxygen mask ensures we can assist others, self-care ensures we're equipped to navigate the challenges of divorce. We have to tend to our wounds before they become infected and cause us and those around us deeper pain and troubles. We must prioritize getting adequate sleep, nourishing food, fresh air, movement, community, and time with God as these are vital pillars of healing.

The Power of Self-Care: Reflect on self-care practices that encompass your physical, emotional, and spiritual well-being. Write about activities that rejuvenate you, offer comfort, and foster growth. Consider how you can prioritize these practices amidst the demands of divorce. By embracing self-care, you demonstrate self-love and accelerate your healing journey—physically, mentally, emotionally, and spiritually.

I Corinthians 6:19-20
Galatians 6:9-10

GUILT

In the wake of divorce, guilt often lingers, regardless of our circumstances. We replay scenarios in our minds, pondering the "if only's" and "what ifs," laden with a burden of remorse. Mistakes are part of being human, yet it's when we allow those mistakes to evolve into labels that shame and guilt pile upon us.

The weight of shame need not be our cross to bear. We could sit here looking at our wounds as we bleed out or we can take action to stop the bleeding and allow healing to begin. It is in our power to redirect our guilt toward healing, allowing it to lead us back to God. Through Him, we can relinquish our burdens, confident that His forgiveness and grace have the strength to dissolve our guilt.

Releasing the Shackles of Guilt: Reflect upon any guilt you've been carrying about the divorce. Journal about your intention to remove these burdens, entrusting them to God's unfailing love and forgiveness. Embrace the freedom that comes from letting go, recognizing that God's grace is sufficient to wash away the stains of guilt. As you unburden yourself, you pave the way for healing and restoration, enabling you to move forward with renewed hope.

Psalm 103:12
Romans 8:1

GOD'S LOVE

The collapse of our marriage casts doubt upon the very nature of love—love that was meant to be enduring, unconditional, and everlasting. In the face of such shattered expectations, it's easy to question love itself, including the love of God. We may find ourselves wondering if anyone could truly love us or why love would be desirable at all. Yet, amidst these uncertainties, one constant remains: God's unchanging love.

The open wound that love has left hurts. Even the thought of someone coming close enough to touch that tender wound can make us flinch. God's love may not be comfortable at first, but it will cleanse the wound and help us to heal.

Even as we navigate the turmoil of divorce, we must recognize that God's love is unwavering. Regardless of our circumstances, past actions, or our current emotional state, God's love remains steadfast. His love is so profound that He willingly offered His Son's life for us. This love surpasses any love we've ever known, and it can restore and transform even in the aftermath of divorce.

Revealing Love's Resilience: Reflect on how your perception of God's love has transformed during the divorce journey. Write about the moments when you've felt His love surrounding you, providing solace, strength, and healing. These experiences remind us that God's love transcends our challenges, offering a love that can mend, renew, and uplift. Through this reflection, you can discover the depths of God's love and allow it to shape your perspective as you move forward with hope and newfound understanding.

Romans 8:38-39
I John 4:9-10

PROFESSIONAL HELP

Admitting our need for help can be an uphill battle, particularly when sharing our deepest fears, worries, and problems with strangers. Professional counseling and therapy can often bear a stigma, and for men, seeking assistance can be even more challenging, especially when sharing emotions isn't our norm.

However, engaging in sessions with a professional can be a transformative step in this journey. While we can Google medical symptoms, only professionals can provide the necessary medication to combat an infection. As we might read up on legal matters, an experienced attorney can be indispensable in a courtroom. Similarly, seeking help from a professional is vital for our mental and emotional well-being.

A skilled professional does more than listen; they genuinely hear us. They pose thoughtful questions, guiding us toward clarity. They challenge us while offering encouragement. Opening up to someone can open doors we hadn't even noticed, allowing us to perceive our situation from a fresh perspective.

The modern age offers flexibility through online and telehealth options. Various websites provide accessible avenues for finding suitable professionals who align with our schedules and needs. Also, apps such as Calm, Headspace, or Pause provide good meditation and breathing exercises.

Embracing the Path to Healing: Consider seeking professional help as part of your healing process. Research online therapy options and explore coverage through your insurance provider. Reflect on any reservations you might have, and outline steps you can take to prioritize your mental health. Remember, seeking assistance doesn't diminish strength; instead, it demonstrates self-awareness and courage on the path to healing.

Proverbs 15:22
Proverbs 11:14
Ecclesiastes 4:9-10

PURPOSE IN PAIN

There is no denying the fact that divorce inflicts deep pain. It's a wound that cuts to the core, leaving an ache that defies attempts at alleviation. Yet, even within this excruciating experience, there lies a potential for transformation, for the pain to be repurposed for God's glory.

During the storm, it's challenging to discern how such a traumatic experience could serve a higher purpose. Yet, we can discover meaning in our pain—a silver lining within the darkness. Our messy, difficult journey through divorce can ultimately become a powerful message of resilience, growth, and faith.

Through the crucible of adversity, we can refine ourselves, emerging from the struggle stronger and more resilient. Our growth equips us to support others who are treading similar paths. In sharing our story, we can uplift, guide, and inspire those navigating their challenges.

Purpose Emerging from Pain: Reflect on how you believe God can weave purpose into your experiences and pain. Journal about any instances where you've glimpsed a higher purpose, even in the midst of your struggles. Consider how you might actively seek and nurture a sense of purpose, leveraging your pain to offer hope and encouragement to others. Through this reflection, you uncover the potential for transformation and discover the beauty that can arise from brokenness.

Romans 8:28
2 Corinthians 1:4
James 1:2-4

STRENGTHENING FAITH

Questioning everything, including our faith, is an instinctive response to the turmoil of divorce. Yet, just as an oak tree's strength is fortified through testing, our faith, too, can be deepened during challenging times. Like the oak tree that bends but doesn't break in the wind, our faith can become more resilient as we anchor ourselves in God's presence.

Similar to how the oak tree widens its roots for stability, we can deepen our relationship with God, seeking solace and strength in Him. In uncertainty, leaning on God becomes an act of trust, allowing Him to guide us through the storm.

Strengthening the Faith Amidst Challenges: Reflect on the steps you're taking to nurture and deepen your relationship with God during this season of divorce. Journal how you're leaning into your faith, seeking comfort, wisdom, and guidance. Whether through prayer, scripture, meditation, or seeking fellowship, note how these practices are grounding you and allowing your faith to grow stronger. By actively cultivating your relationship with God, you can find a source of unwavering support and renewal during the storm.

Hebrews 11:1
Romans 10:17
I Peter 1:6-7

NEW BEGINNING

As the lyrics from the 90s one hit wonder Semisonic's 'Closing Time' remind us, "Every new beginning comes from some other beginning's end." With the closing of our marriage, we're turning the page on a chapter that was once our life's blueprint. While we may have envisioned it as a complete book, we must acknowledge that it was, in fact, a chapter—one that ended unexpectedly.

While it's tempting to linger in what could have been, doing so offers us little benefit. Longing for an alternate reality doesn't serve our growth. This juncture signifies a new beginning, a fresh canvas to paint our future. The slate has been wiped clean, and while the future may not align with our initial plans, it doesn't negate the potential for a remarkable journey ahead.

This moment heralds the advent of new possibilities and opportunities previously concealed. As our wound heals it may leave a scar that can help to tell an overcoming story. The dawn of this new chapter empowers us to sculpt an excellent future, one that may have been beyond our imagination during our previous beginning.

Embracing the Uncharted Future: Journal about the possibilities that beckon and the opportunities that lie ahead. Explore the dreams and ideas that can now be pursued in this newfound chapter. Approach the horizon with hope and anticipation, recognizing that this new beginning presents avenues for growth, fulfillment, and the realization of aspirations you may not have previously entertained. By embracing the unknown with optimism, you set the stage for a future shaped by your vision and choices. What are some dreams and ideas that you can now pursue in this new beginning? How can you approach the future with hope and anticipation?

Isaiah 43:19
2 Corinthians 5:17
Lamentations 3:22-23

MENDING

Ernest Hemingway's words from 'A Farewell to Arms" resonate deeply: "The world breaks everyone, and afterward, many are stronger at the broken places." This sentiment undoubtedly applies to us as we stand here today. Divorce inevitably brings about brokenness; it's an undeniable facet of our journey. However, it's essential to recognize that experiencing a break doesn't label us as broken individuals. Instead, it signifies an opportunity for healing and growth.

As broken bones mend and fractured pieces can be reassembled, our shattered aspects can be restored. The journey of healing can lead us to emerge even stronger with newfound wisdom and resilience. Often, it's those who rise from their falls, mending their fractures, who go on to achieve remarkable feats and inspire others.

In this journey, we're not alone. Our greatest Healer, the Lord, is ever-present. If we entrust our broken hearts to Him, He can mend them. Through His grace, He can transform our pain into strength, our wounds into wisdom, and our brokenness into a testament to His healing power.

Healing and Wholeness in God's Care: Reflect on the areas of brokenness in your life—emotional, spiritual, or otherwise. Journal how you can consciously surrender these areas to God's healing touch. Consider how you can actively seek His restoration, allowing Him to mend the broken places and make you even stronger than before. Through this process, you can discover the transformative power of God's love and healing in your life.

Psalm 147:3
Isaiah 61:1

FAITHFULNESS

Divorce encompasses a multitude of life's facets, and likening it to a storm is an apt and relatable analogy. It's as if we're adrift in a boat on a stormy sea, enveloped by howling winds, crashing waves, and relentless rain. Amidst the darkness, punctuated by flashes of lightning, we navigate the uncertainty, often unsure of our direction.

This scene evokes the imagery of the apostles facing a similar predicament. They were in a boat during a storm, panic and fear gripping them, even though Jesus was present with them. Their experience mirrors our own emotions of fear and feeling lost. In the story, Jesus was asleep in the boat until he was awakened by the apostles' distress. His rebuke silenced the storm, and He turned to His disciples, questioning their fear and lack of faith.

Faith doesn't exempt us from facing storms; instead, it assures us that we have Jesus to lean on during these tumultuous times. Our journey through divorce can indeed test our faith. However, rather than questioning or turning away from God, we can choose to see His faithfulness shining through the storm.

Witnessing God's Unfailing Faithfulness: Reflect on the instances of God's faithfulness you've encountered throughout the divorce process. Journal how His presence has provided sustenance and solace, offering a steady anchor amid the chaos. Recognize and celebrate the moments when His guidance, comfort, and provision were palpable, reaffirming that even during life's storms, His faithfulness remains unwavering. Through this reflection, you can cultivate a deeper trust and gratitude for God's presence amid adversity.

Lamentations 3:22-23
I Corinthians 1:9
II Timothy 2:13

FUTURE

The future we once envisioned and held close to our hearts has slipped through our fingers, leaving us with a canvas that resembles a muddled mess of paints on the floor rather than the masterpiece we had hoped for. The Sistine Chapel of our plans now appears transformed into an abstract blur that we would not refer to as art.

In this present moment, uncertainty shrouds our path. The questions about our future echo in our minds, casting doubt on our current circumstances and even the validity of our past. Amid this upheaval, divorce's presence is not what God desires for us, yet we can hold fast to the assurance that God's redemptive power can transform what was intended for harm into something good.

The immediate days ahead are clouded with fear and ambiguity as we grapple with the obscurity of the future. However, by inviting God to work within us, upon us, and through us, we open ourselves to the potential of a future that is not only promising but also overflowing with God's grace and purpose.

Placing Trust in God's Unseen Plan: Delve into the fears and uncertainties that may overshadow your future vision. Journal how you can intentionally release these worries and trust God's greater plan for your life. As you do so, acknowledge that while the future remains unknown, it is well within God's capable hands. This shift in perspective allows you to cultivate peace and anticipation, trusting that God's plan is ultimately unfolding for your good and His glory.

Jeremiah 29:11
Proverbs 3:5-6

LESSONS LEARNED

Every experience we encounter in life serves as an opportunity to grow, strengthen, and accumulate knowledge. Within the crucible of trials, we forge inner strength. Through our interactions with others and the world around us, we glean valuable insights into the human experience—both theirs and ours.

Each experience leaves an indelible mark on our perception. With every encounter, our knowledge base expands, casting fresh light on the world we inhabit. This newfound wisdom can shift our perspective, altering how we view and engage with life.

When we consciously shift our perspective, we unveil a transformative power. Our changed vantage point allows us to perceive life's nuances more clearly—discerning what genuinely matters while letting go of unreasonable concerns. By redirecting our focus to significant truths, we enter a realm where our outlook influences our reality.

Amidst the trials and tribulations of divorce, valuable lessons are ripe for the taking. As we pause to reflect, we can gain insights that transcend the pain and difficulties. This journey is a crucible of transformation, providing us with the chance not only to learn but also to glean wisdom that can reshape our understanding of life.

Shifting Perspective to Embrace Growth: Reflect on the lessons or insights you have gathered from the divorce experience. Journal about how these discoveries have colored your perspective. Consider how shifting your perspective has the potential to illuminate new paths forward and engender a sense of empowerment. Through this process, you can leverage your experiences not only to heal but also to enrich your journey toward a more enlightened and fulfilling future.

Psalm 25:4-5
Proverbs 1:7

HONORING GOD

Even amid the deepest darkness and the most challenging moments of our lives, the choice to live with honor remains within our grasp. In the face of adversity and opposition, we can embody our faith and trust God. Instead of succumbing to the urge to assign blame, we can exercise humility and embrace the wisdom that aligns with God's teachings.

True character shines most brightly during times of crisis. The everyday habits we've cultivated, the principles we've internalized, and the actions we've practiced in private manifest in our thoughts, words, and deeds when we're under pressure. This is how we live a life of integrity.

During the complex and arduous season we find ourselves in, we are called to lean on God's strength, to place our trust in His providence, and to draw deep from our well of faith. Navigating these stormy waters necessitates Godly wisdom, as well as a steadfast commitment to living an honorable life even when circumstances challenge us.

As we strive to honor God through our actions, we can reflect on the wisdom shared in James 3:13 NLT: "If you are wise and understand God's ways, prove it by living an honorable life, doing good works in the humility that comes from wisdom."

Living with Godly Integrity: Reflect on how you can actively integrate your faith into your actions to live with integrity post-divorce. Journal about the decisions you can make, the relationships you can cultivate, and how you can continually grow while remaining aligned with God's teachings. By committing to an honorable life, you not only demonstrate your faith but also inspire those around you with the transformative power of God's wisdom and grace.

I Corinthians 10:31
Colossians 3:17

SURRENDERING BITTERNESS

In this tumultuous period, it's only human to experience a range of painful emotions. The hurt, anger, bitterness, and resentment that may arise are natural responses to the circumstances. Yet, as human beings with the capacity for choice and growth, it's essential to differentiate between feeling these emotions and acting upon them.

Acknowledging our emotions and giving them a name grants us the power to transform our reactions into proactive responses. By recognizing what we feel and labeling our emotions, we open the door to understanding their origins. This understanding, in turn, empowers us to take constructive steps toward healing and resolution.

As these complex emotions surface, it's vital to engage in a process of introspection. By identifying the root causes of our feelings, we pave the way for productive transformation. Confronting our emotions head-on allows us to make a conscious decision—to either harbor resentment indefinitely or embark on a journey of release and healing.

Holding onto bitterness, resentment, and anger is akin to clutching onto a metaphorical rattlesnake, hoping someone else will feel the venomous sting. Alternatively, we can opt for a path of healing and growth. This involves addressing these emotions, permitting ourselves to release them, and embracing the power of forgiveness. By relinquishing these negative emotions, we free ourselves from their grip and open ourselves up to the possibility of a brighter future.

Embracing Emotional Freedom: Reflect on lingering bitterness or resentment towards your ex-spouse. Consider the roots of these emotions and how they have influenced your journey. Journal about the steps to release these emotions and find a path to healing and forgiveness. In doing so, you empower yourself to move forward with renewed strength, emotional freedom, and a heart unburdened by negativity.

Ephesians 4:31-32

STRENGTH IN VULNERABILITY

Vulnerability is a word that often evokes strong reactions, whether positive or negative. However, during this challenging journey, embracing vulnerability becomes essential—though it's important to exercise discernment in sharing our innermost thoughts and feelings.

While it might be tempting to broadcast every emotion and concern on social media, this is a time to be selective. Rather than casting our vulnerability widely, we can confide in a few trusted individuals. These are the people who truly understand us, who offer a safe space for us to open up, and who support our healing process. These connections are invaluable—providing a refuge to remove our masks, pour out our hearts, express our struggles, and find solace.

Amid the thick fog of this chapter in our lives, vulnerability becomes a lifeline. By sharing our burdens and emotions, we prevent them from accumulating and eventually exploding. These trusted individuals become our pillars of strength—lifting us up when we stumble, helping us find our footing, and holding us accountable when our focus wavers.

By embracing vulnerability with care and wisdom, we not only release the weight of our emotions but also cultivate deeper, more meaningful connections. It's within these connections that we discover the power of human empathy, compassion, and the shared human experience. Vulnerability fosters healing, forging bonds that can support us through the toughest of times.

Nurturing Deeper Connections: Reflect on the individuals you can trust and confide in during this journey. Journal about the strength that vulnerability brings to these relationships and how sharing your challenges and emotions can lead to mutual support and healing. By being discerning and intentional with our vulnerability, we create spaces of genuine connection and understanding.

2 Corinthians 12:9-10
Psalm 34:17-18

CELEBRATING PROGRESS

This journey embarked from a place of darkness, turmoil, and misery. While the path has been arduous, it's crucial to acknowledge what we've navigated through, overcoming obstacles and achieving victories along the way.

Through the challenges, we've managed to evolve and better ourselves. Our faith has deepened, revealing a stronger connection with the Divine. We've embarked on a journey of self-discovery, unearthing layers of our identity. We've honed skills and talents, conquering hurdles that once seemed impossible. Our determination and surrender to God's shaping hands have molded us into men of resilience and strength.

The vision of our future may have shifted from what we once envisioned, but it's a future filled with promise and brightness. The storm may still be present, but our progress cannot be denied. Despite facing setbacks and defeats, we've refused to succumb. Along this road, we've reached significant milestones and tasted the sweetness of victories, both large and small.

In celebrating our progress, we acknowledge the miles we've traversed. Each step forward is a testament to our tenacity, our faith, and the transformative power of resilience. Let's rejoice in our growth and accomplishments as we chart our course through this storm, emerging even stronger on the other side.

Marking Milestones: Reflect on the victories, both personal and spiritual, that you have achieved since the beginning of this journey. Journal about how each success has shaped your perspective and propelled you forward. Acknowledging our progress, we embrace the transformative nature of challenges and triumphs.

Philippians 1:6

EMBRACING HOPE

One day, atop a majestic mountain, we shall stand. The sun's warm embrace will envelop us, and the air will carry a pristine freshness that invigorates our very being. At that moment, we shall gaze around, and the darkness of our current valley will have receded into the distant horizon, a mere speck in the vastness.

Our future is a beacon of radiance, teeming with promise. Even in the midst of uncertainty and when the dreams of tomorrow remain veiled, we stand here today, catching a glimpse of our future selves. It's a vision of us living life abundantly and unapologetically. Fueled by hope, we chase dreams that have long slumbered within us, awakening them to vibrant life.

In this vision, we paint our future with hues of brilliance, crafting a tapestry of a life that resonates with purpose and beauty. The path ahead is illuminated by the unwavering faithfulness of God, whose promises guide us through the unknown. With each step, we journey deeper into a life fully lived, rooted in the knowledge that Jesus has come, that we might experience life in its entirety.

As we stand on the cusp of what's to come, let us embrace the wisdom of embracing the present moment. Let gratitude fill our hearts for the lessons of the past and the blessings of today. In this act, we find strength to carry us forward, shaping the narrative of our lives.

The future is a blank canvas, a masterpiece awaiting the strokes of our aspirations and endeavors. With every brushstroke, we infuse it with our unique essence, co-creating with our God that created us. And as we breathe life into our dreams, we recognize that the journey is as significant as the destination.

Embrace the struggles, for they are the crucible through which resilience is forged. Embrace the victories, for they affirm the strength residing within. In both the triumphs and challenges, the beauty of life is woven.

As we move ahead, remember that our true nature thrives in the face of adversity. With God's grace as our anchor, we navigate the seas of uncertainty guided by the compass of faith. Each step forward affirms hope, a declaration that the future is a canvas waiting to be adorned.

Hold dear the promise of a future painted with moments of joy, purpose, and grace. Embrace the fullness of life, for the journey itself is a testimony to God's faithfulness. Let this vision be a sanctuary of courage when the path is steep and a sanctuary of hope when clouds gather.

With unwavering belief in what's to come, step forward, my dear soul, knowing that each day unfolds with the possibility of miracles. The mountaintop is ahead, the sun has risen, and a life lived fully awaits.

Embracing Hope: Write a letter to your future self, expressing your hopes and dreams for the journey ahead. Offer words of encouragement and remind yourself of God's faithfulness.

Romans 15:13
Jeremiah 29:11

Dear Future Me,

As I write this letter, I am excited about your incredible journey ahead. I want you to know that I believe in you wholeheartedly, and I'm sending my hopes and dreams for you into the future.

I imagine you standing on that mountaintop, basking in the warmth of the sun's embrace. The struggles and storms of the past will be like distant memories fading into the background. The air around you will be pure and invigorating, a reflection of the renewed spirit within you.

I know you are living a life bursting with hope and vitality. You've embraced the dreams that once resided deep within your heart, turning them into reality with the strength and determination that you possess. Your journey may have been challenging, but those challenges have sculpted you into who you are today.

Remember that your future is as bright as the promises of God. He has been faithful through every twist and turn, and He will continue to be your guiding light as you forge ahead. Your relationship with Him has deepened, and your faith has become an unbreakable foundation.

Embrace every moment, whether big or small, with gratitude and enthusiasm. Keep your eyes fixed on the path before you, allowing God's grace to lead you. Embrace the beauty in each day, for life is a precious gift meant to be lived fully.

Always hold onto the truth that you are loved, cherished, and designed for greatness. Your journey has been one of growth, and your future is a canvas waiting to be painted with vibrant and meaningful experiences.

Believe in yourself, for you are stronger than you know. Keep your heart open to new possibilities, and don't be afraid to step out of your comfort zone. Remember that you have the power to create a life that aligns with your deepest values and dreams.

May your future be filled with joy, purpose, and a heart that continues to seek and share love. Keep shining your light, for the world needs your unique brilliance. With God by your side, there is nothing you cannot overcome.

I send you all my love, encouragement, and unwavering faith as you journey upward, onward, and ever forward!

With hope and anticipation,

Me

My brother, we have made great strides along the path and have dealt with many monsters along the way. Yet, this is not the end of the journey. We must continue to press on. To fight on.

We may need to take another walk through this journal or face a few of the tougher, more challenging prompts again in order for us to seek further healing as we strive to become all He created us to be, as we strive to live life to the full as He has promised.

You have shown strength and fortitude facing these difficulties head on. You have shared your deepest pains and thoughts with me. Thank you for your honesty and openness. It hasn't been easy, but it has been worth it.

I appreciate your willingness to walk with me and allow me to walk by your side as we navigated this difficult path. I pray that what we have endured has made us stronger and better.

I am proud of you. I love you brother!